I was diagnosed with schizophrenia and ASD at the age of 18. I have used art as a coping mechanism and an escape for as long as I can remember, but now I want to help people not only to understand mental health, but to accept it as well.

STORY OF LARRY

Hi I'm Larry
I have
schizophrenia.

ADAM BROMILEY-HASLAM

AUSTIN MACAULEY PUBLISHERS™
LONDON • CAMBRIDGE • NEW YORK • SHARJAH

A CIP catalogue record for this title is available from the British Library.

ISBN 9781035820771 (Paperback)
ISBN 9781035820788 (ePub e-book)

www.austinmacauley.com

First Published 2024
Austin Macauley Publishers Ltd®
1 Canada Square
Canary Wharf
London
E14 5AA

Larry sometimes sees things that aren't real; this is a hallucination.

It's very confusing!

Larry might hear voices. These voices can be very demanding and tell him to do things.

Feed me!

He might even start talking to the fish!

Lovely weather we're having Larry.

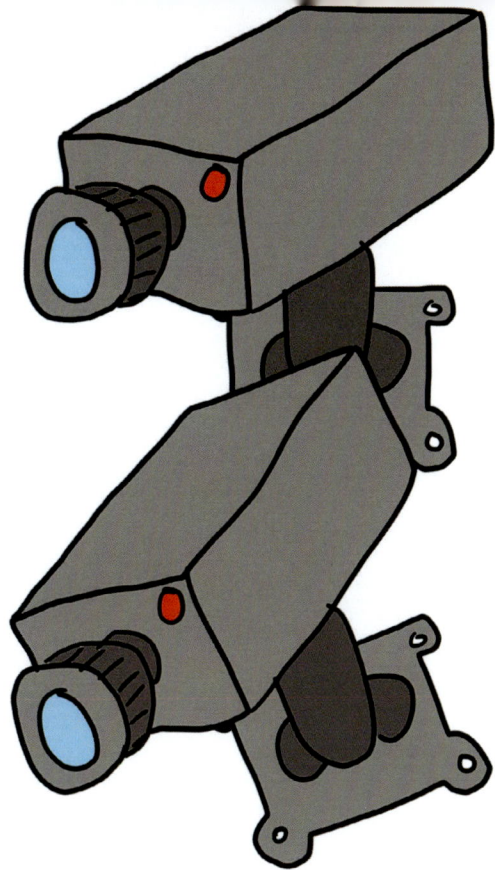

Larry might have delusions. This can be scary and intimidating for Larry.

Delusions can make Larry very paranoid and aware of people.

These delusions can be good and bad!

Larry's speech can sometimes get muddled up. This is called "WORD SALAD".

He might not make that much sense.

His thoughts can also be affected.

Larry finds it really difficult to show his feelings. This is the blunted affect. It will be hard for Larry.

Larry might have trouble sleeping. Even counting sheep doesn't help.

There are many ways to manage schizophrenia.

The most common ways are therapy and medication.

Understanding this illness can be very difficult, so loving friends and family will help Larry fight this never-ending battle.

Larry is very scared because his thoughts appear real. This could make Larry very paranoid and aware of his surroundings.

The paranoia and the confusion of this illness might make Larry become secluded

Another cause of paranoia and anxiety are the
"INTRUSIVE THOUGHTS".
These are involuntary thoughts and can be very repetitive and distressing.

WHAT IF?

Intrusive thoughts can progress into "OCD".

This book has been written from my own experience with schizophrenia, it is a battle everyday

Thankyou Larry for opening up and explaining some signs of schizophrenia!!

This book might seem simple, but I have experienced the very thing that makes you question reality. The countless mental battles, fighting no one but yourself. The constant fear of being alone. But, if I can reach just one person_

"I'd do it all again"